St. Thomas and Port Stanley Ontario in Colour Photos, Saving Our History One Photo at a Time

Photography
by Barbara Raué
2014

Series Name:
Cruising Ontario

Book 49: St. Thomas and Port Stanley

Cover photo: 1 Wellington Street, St. Thomas – built 1878
(McLachlin House) - Queen Anne style
– turrets, scroll work, bracketing, dormers

Series Name: Cruising Ontario
Saving Our History One Photo at a Time

Other Books by Barbara Raue

Coins of Gold

Arrows, Indians and Love

The Life and Times of Barbara
Volume 1: Inventions That Have Enhanced My Life
Volume 2: Entertainment That I Have Enjoyed
Volume 3: East Coast Trips
Volume 4: Olympics Have Always Intrigued Me
Volume 5: Wonders of the World
Volume 6: Caribbean Cruises We Have Enjoyed
Volume 7: Animals
Volume 8: Storms and Other Major Disasters in My Lifetime
Volume 9: Wars, Terrorist Attacks and Major Disasters

The Cromwell Family Book

Laura Secord Discovered

Visit Barbara's website to view all of her books
http://barbararaue.ericraue.com

St. Thomas

Colonel The Honourable Thomas Talbot (1771-1853), the founder of the "Talbot Settlement", was born at Castle Malahide, Ireland. In 1803, after serving in the British Army, he was granted 5,000 acres and settled in Dunwich Township. He promoted colonization by building mills, supervising the construction of a three hundred mile long road paralleling Lake Erie, and helping establish thousands of settlers in the area. In 1817 St. Thomas, located south of London and north of Port Stanley, was named for him.

St. Thomas, located in Southwestern Ontario at the intersection of two historical roads, was first settled in 1810. It was named the seat of the new Elgin County in 1844 and became a city in 1881.

The founder of the settlement that became St. Thomas was Captain Daniel Rapelje. In 1820, Rapelje divided his land into town lots for a village. He donated two acres of land for the building of Old St. Thomas Church.

In 1871, the developing village of Millersburg, which included lands east of the London and Port Stanley Railway, amalgamated with St. Thomas.

In the late nineteenth century and early twentieth century several railways were constructed through the city and St. Thomas became an important railway junction. A total of twenty-six railways have passed through the city since the first railway was completed in 1856. In the 1950s and 1960s, with the decline of the railway as a mode of transportation, other industry began to locate in the city, mainly primary and secondary automotive manufacturing.

In 1824, Charles Duncombe and John Rolph established the first medical school in Upper Canada, in St. Thomas, under the patronage of Colonel Thomas Talbot. Duncombe's house now forms part of The Elgin Military Museum complex. Between 1881 and 1988 the city had a private woman's school operating called Alma College which was destroyed by fire in 2008.

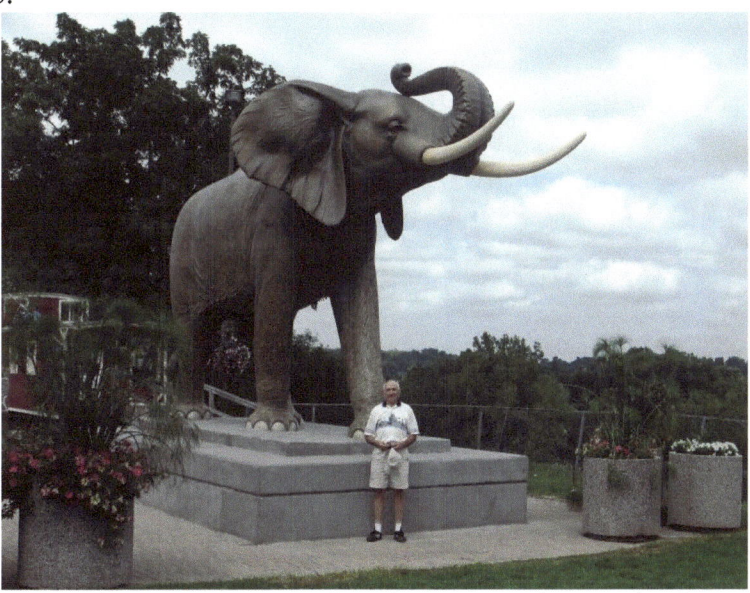

On September 15, 1885, Jumbo, the giant African elephant, star of the Barnum & Bailey Circus, met an untimely death when struck in St. Thomas by a Grand Trunk locomotive. The life-size commemorative statue was erected in 1985.

Port Stanley

Lieutenant-Colonel John Bostwick – 1780-1849 – Born in Massachusetts, Bostwick came as a child to Norfolk County. He was appointed high constable of the London District in 1800 and sheriff in 1805. A deputy-surveyor, he laid out some of the earliest roads in the Talbot Settlement and in 1804 was granted 600 acres at the mouth of Kettle Creek. After serving as a militia officer throughout the War of 1812, he settled on the site of Port Stanley and founded this community. Bostwick represented Middlesex in the legislative assembly 1821-24. He donated the land for this church, which was completed in 1845, and he is buried in its churchyard.

Port Stanley is located on the north shore of Lake Erie at the mouth of Kettle Creek. It was part of an important early route from Lake Erie to other inland waterways for a succession of explorers and travellers of the seventeenth and eighteenth centuries, serving as an important landing point and camping spot. Adrien Jolliet, brother of Louis Jolliet, landed here in 1669 during the first descent of the Great Lakes by Europeans.

A settlement named Kettle Creek was founded here in 1812 by Lieutenant-Colonel John Bostwick. Around 1824, it was renamed Port Stanley after Edward Smith-Stanley, 14th Earl of Derby, who had visited nearby Port Talbot. Lord Stanley later became Prime Minister of the United Kingdom and the father of Frederick Stanley, 16th Earl of Derby, Governor General of Canada, and an ice hockey enthusiast and donor of the first Stanley Cup in 1893.

St. Thomas

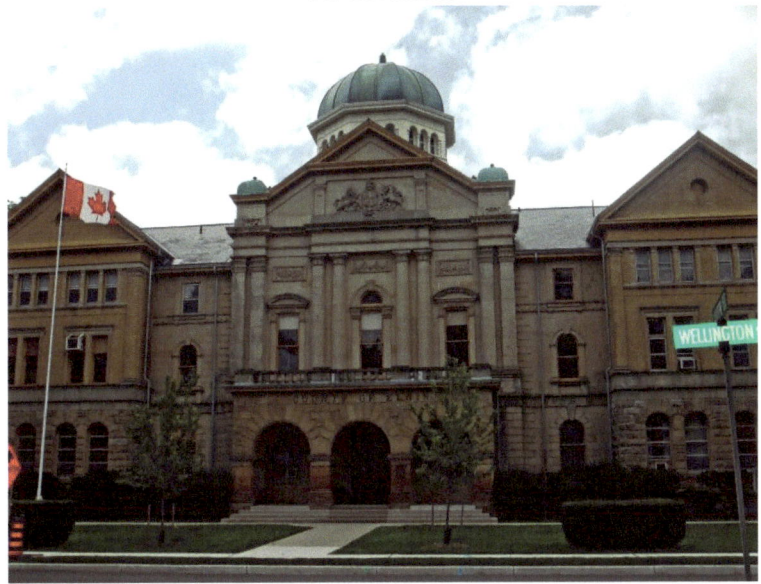

Elgin County Court House – Victorian style architecture

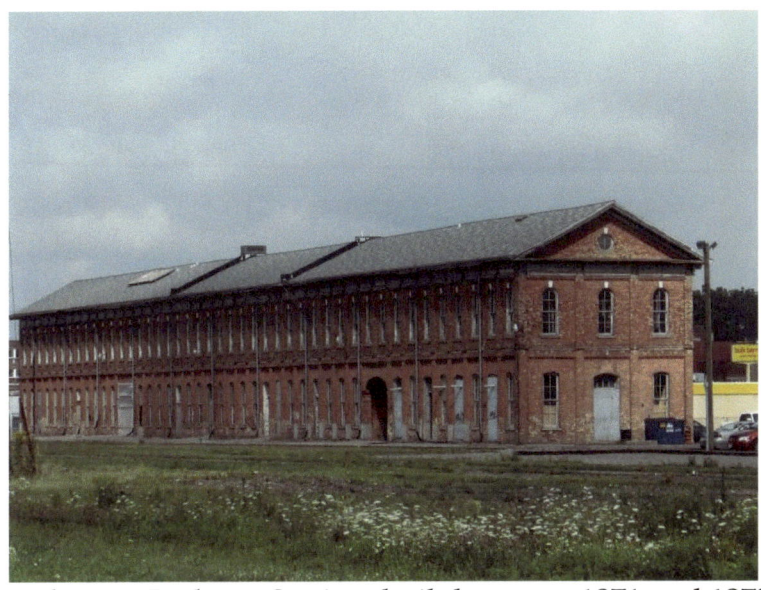

St. Thomas Railway Station, built between 1871 and 1873, is currently being restored

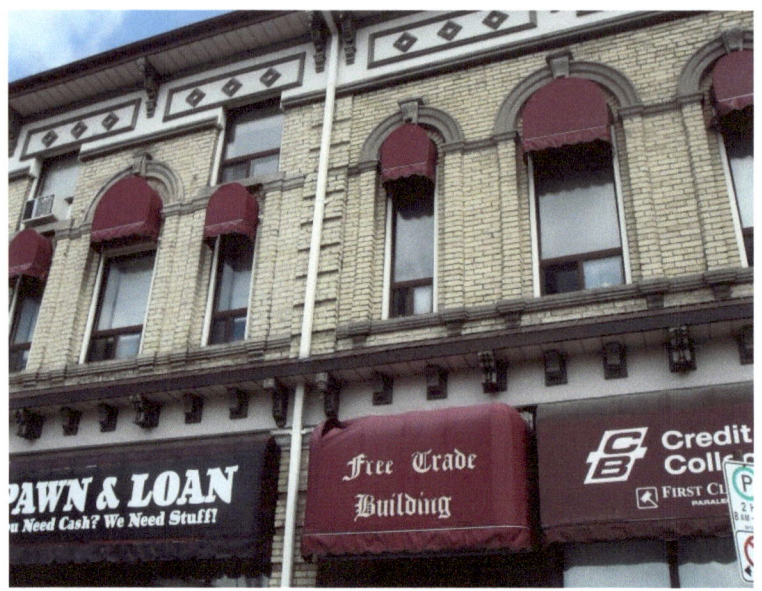

Arched window voussoirs with keystones

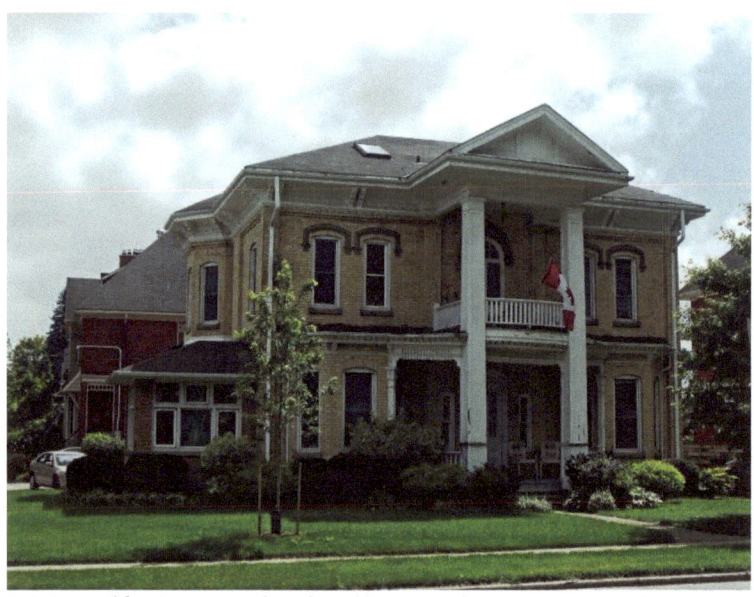

91 Metcalfe Street – built 1871 - Italianate – single cornice brackets, pediment above second floor balcony, arched voussoirs, Greek Revival porch supported by Ionic columns

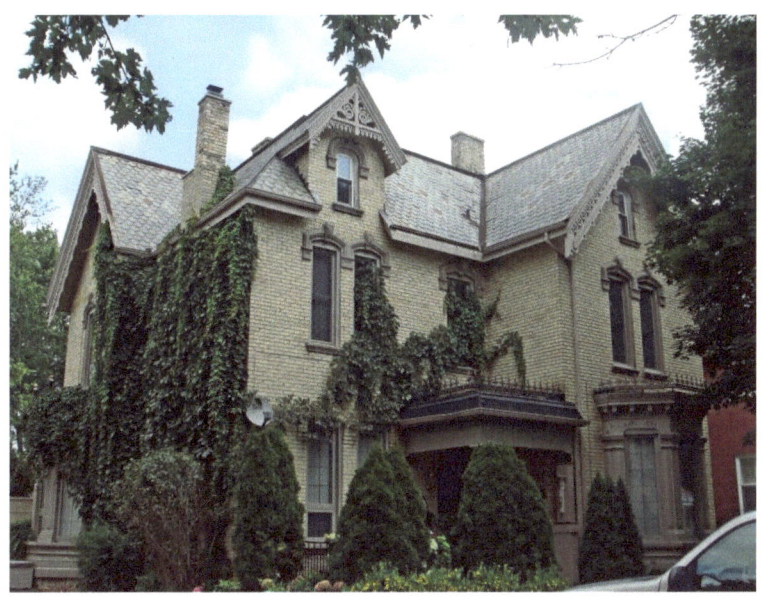

13 Wellington Street – built in 1881 - Gothic Revival – ornate Vergeboard on dormer and extending wing, roof is surfaced in patterned slate, iron cresting above bay window and above porch, elaborate stone eyebrows surmount the paired windows on the second floor

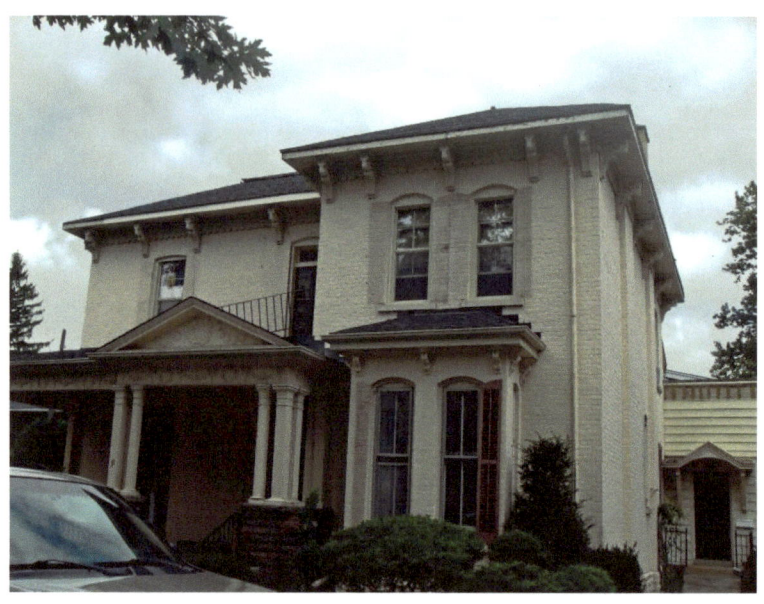

9 Wellington Street – Italianate, built 1878 – hip roof, single cornice brackets, square bay window located in the projecting wing on the right
– porch is classic Greek with decorated pediment

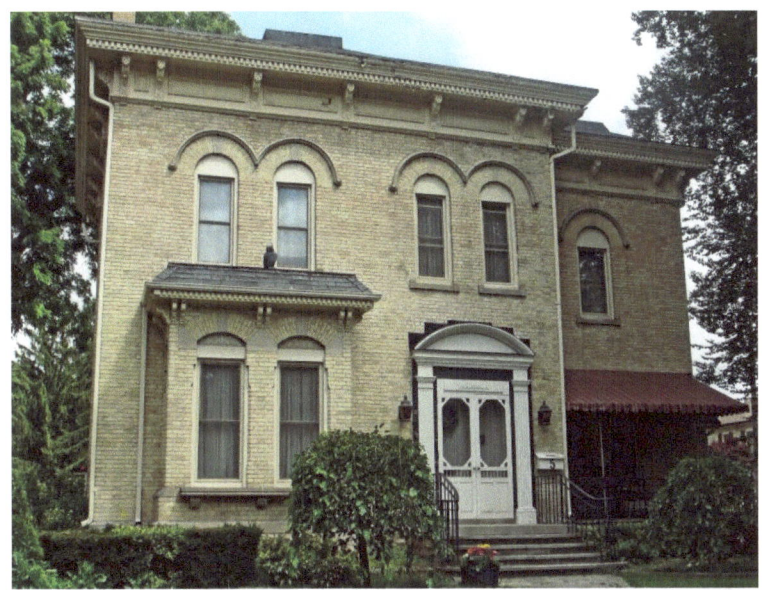

5 Wellington Street – built 1878 – two-storey brick Italianate style – hip roof, single cornice brackets, rounded windows with eyebrow inserts of cut stone

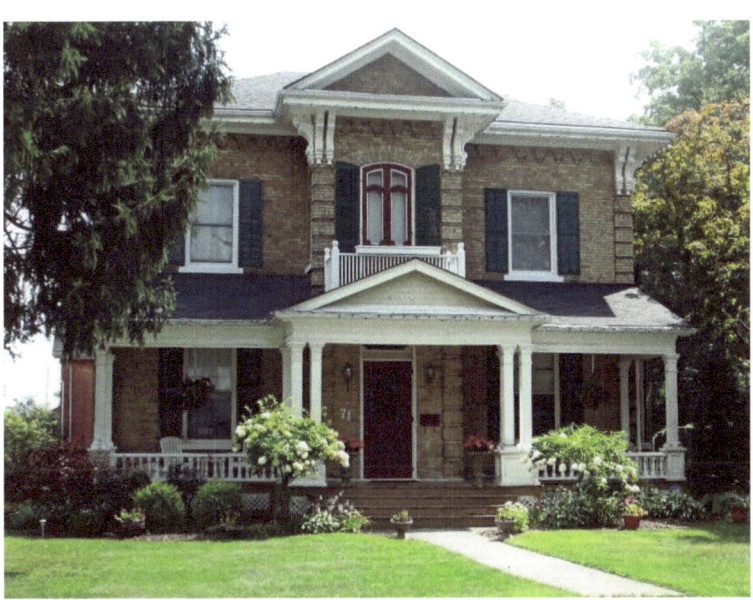

71 Metcalfe Street – Georgian with three-bay front, the centre bay projects forward, pediment, cornice brackets

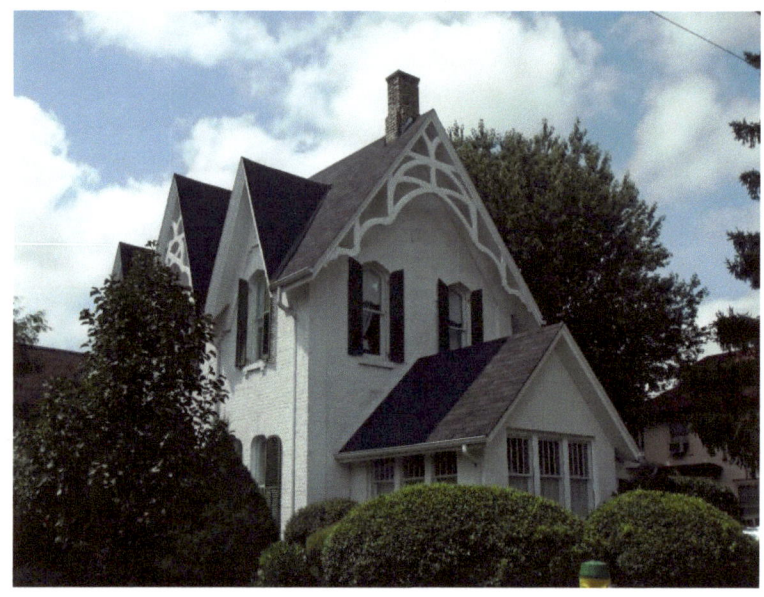

72 Metcalfe Street – built in 1875 - Gothic Revival – sharply peaked roof, intricate Vergeboard trim

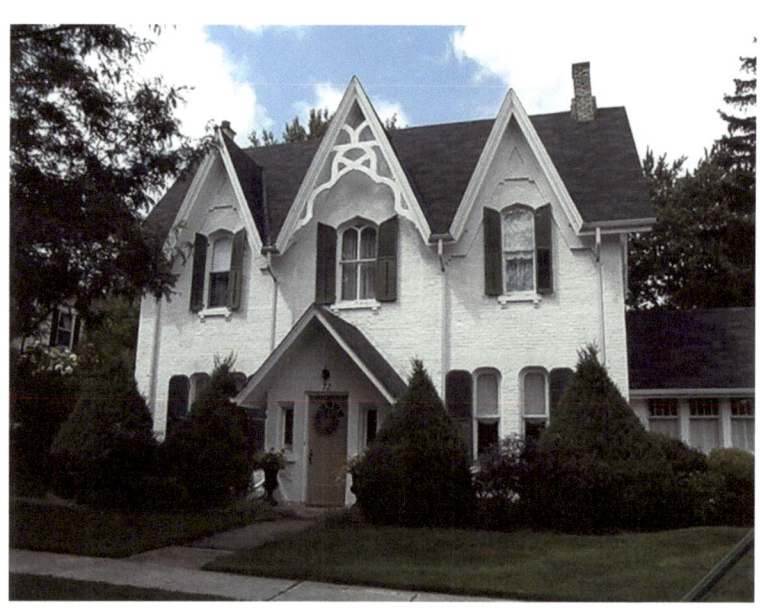

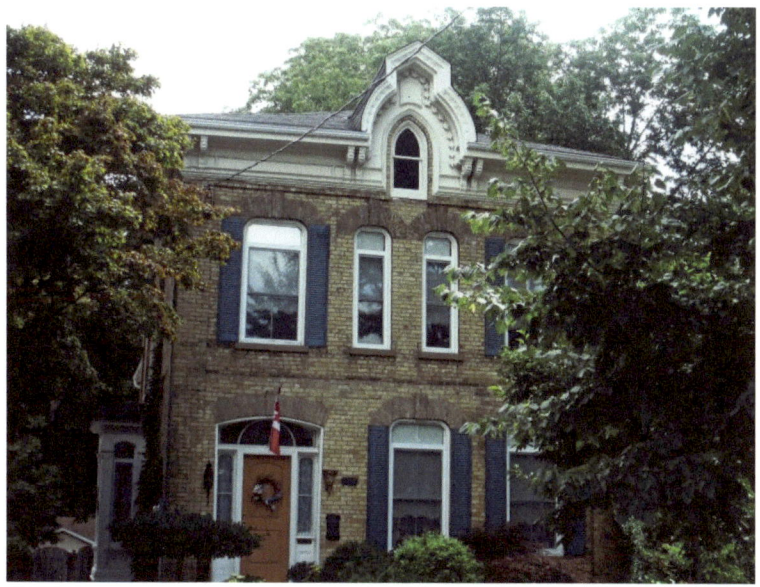

73 Metcalfe Street – built 1875 - Italianate – uniquely shaped centre gable with arched window at the attic level

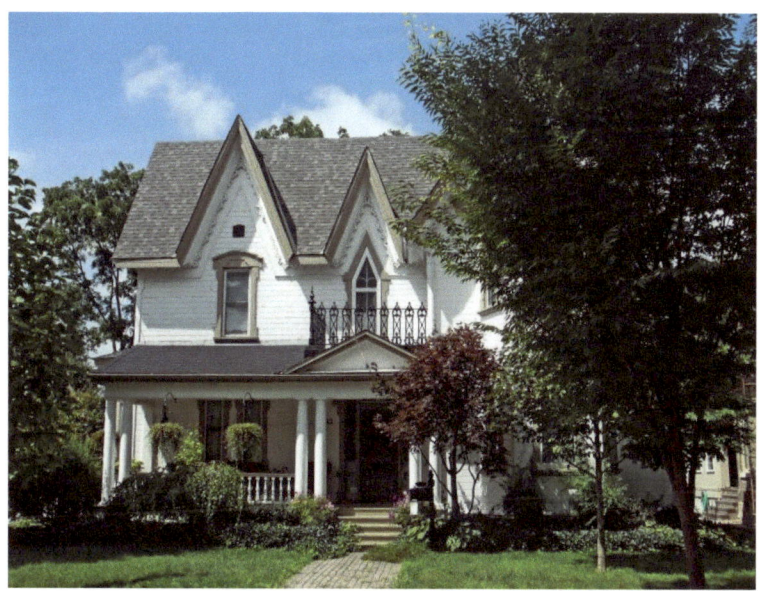

92 Metcalfe – built 1875 – two-storey frame Gothic house with a three peaked roof, Doric columns with pediment, iron cresting on verandah roof

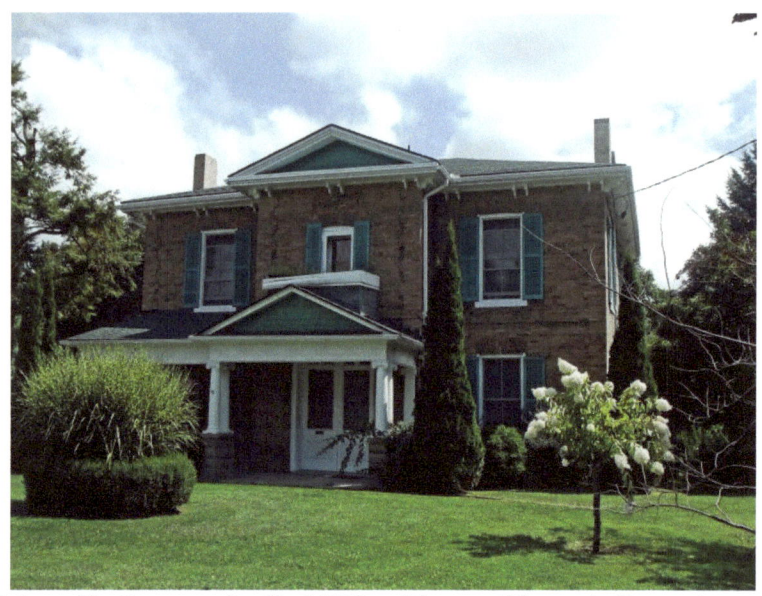

95 Metcalfe Street – built 1858 – (Coyne House) Georgian with two-storey frontispiece topped with a pediment, paired cornice brackets, hipped roof

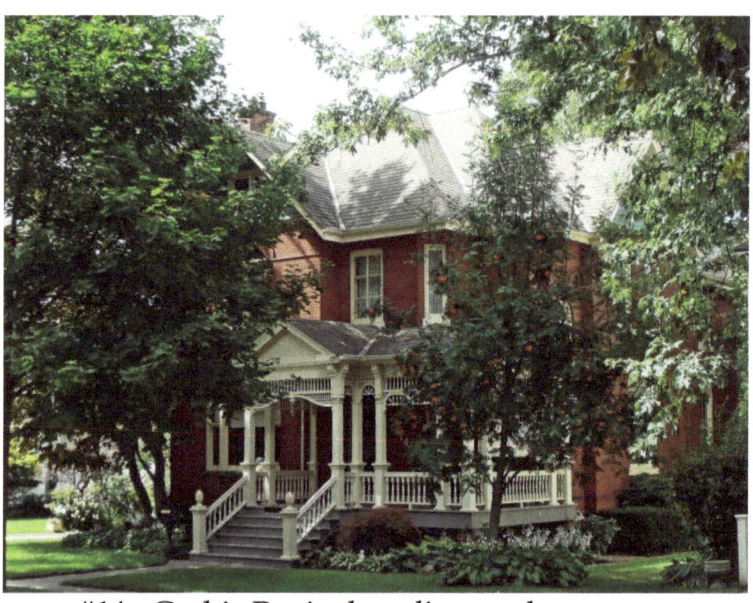

#14 - Gothic Revival, pediment above steps

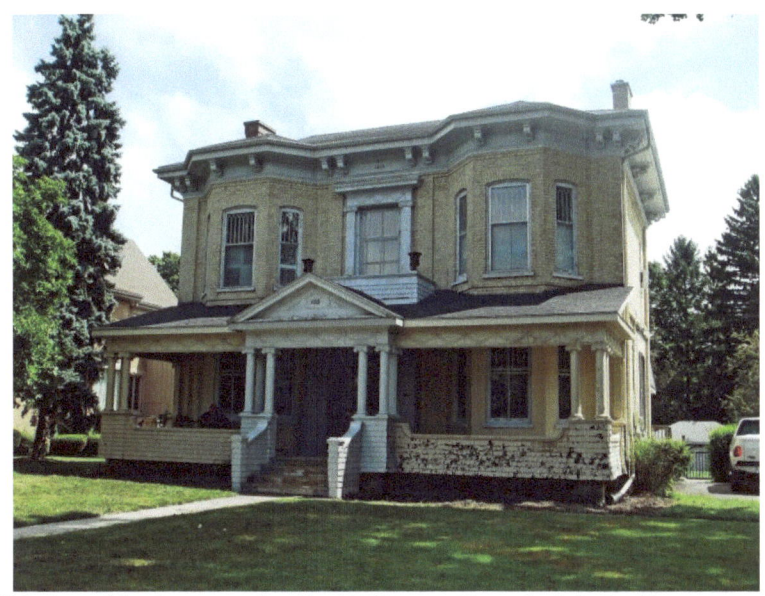

105 Metcalfe Street – built 1872 – yellow brick Italianate with
two-storey bay windows, paired cornice brackets, pediment
above door, full width veranda with Ionic columns

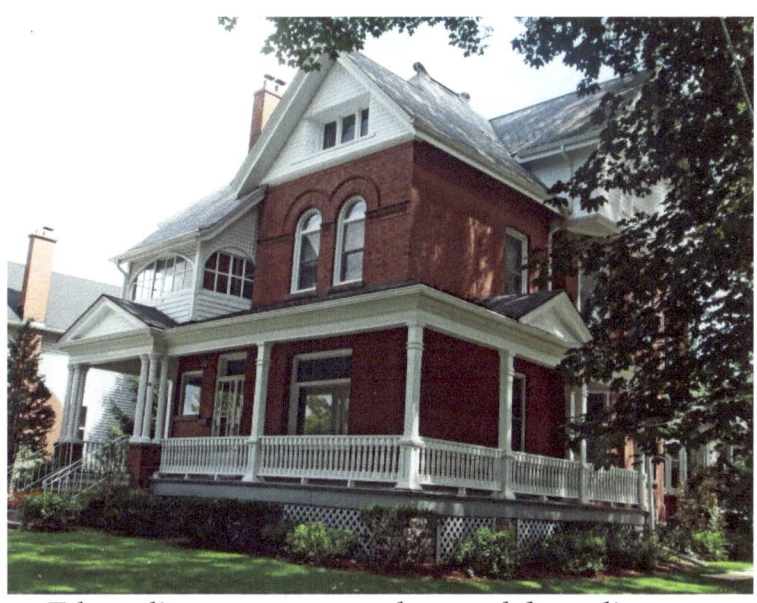

Edwardian – wraparound verandah, pediments,
Romanesque style round-arched voussoirs

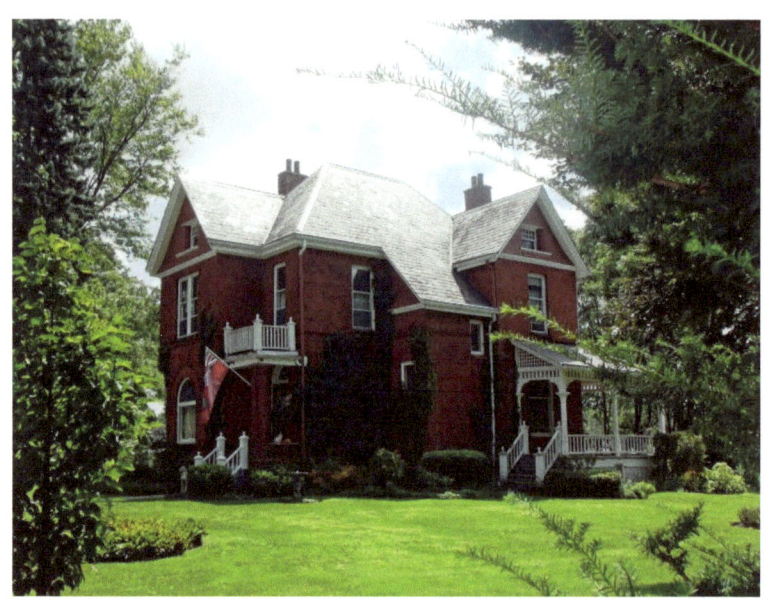

Gothic Revival, balcony on second floor, round Romanesque style window voussoirs on ground floor

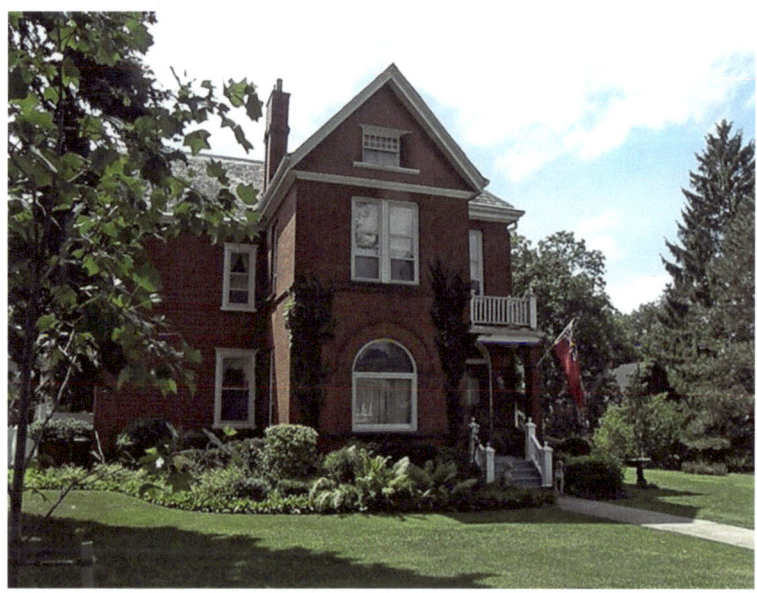

Romanesque-style arched window voussoir

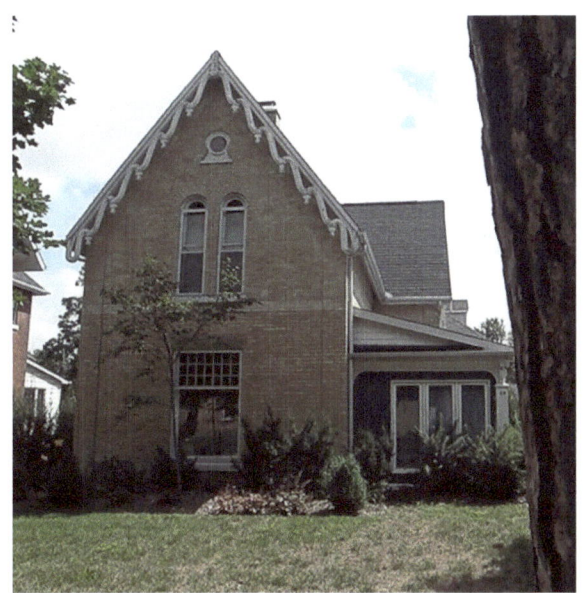

Gothic Revival – Vergeboard trim on gable

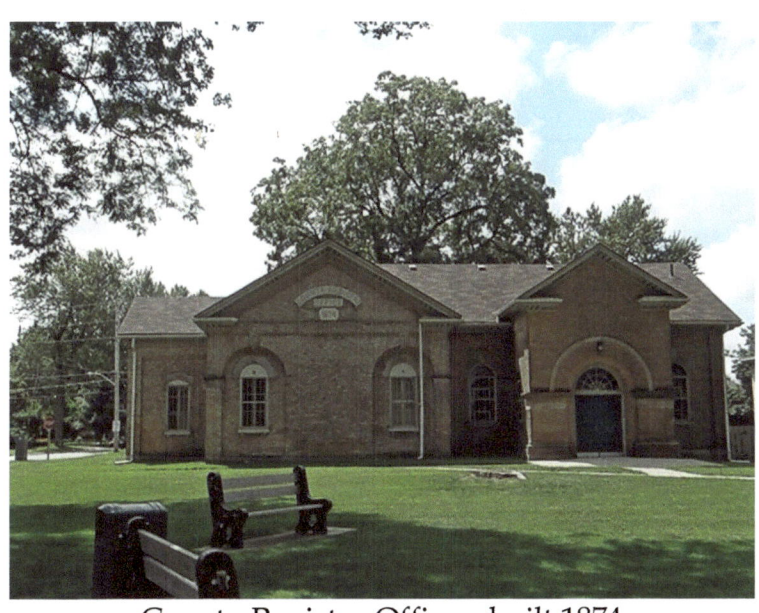

County Registry Office – built 1874

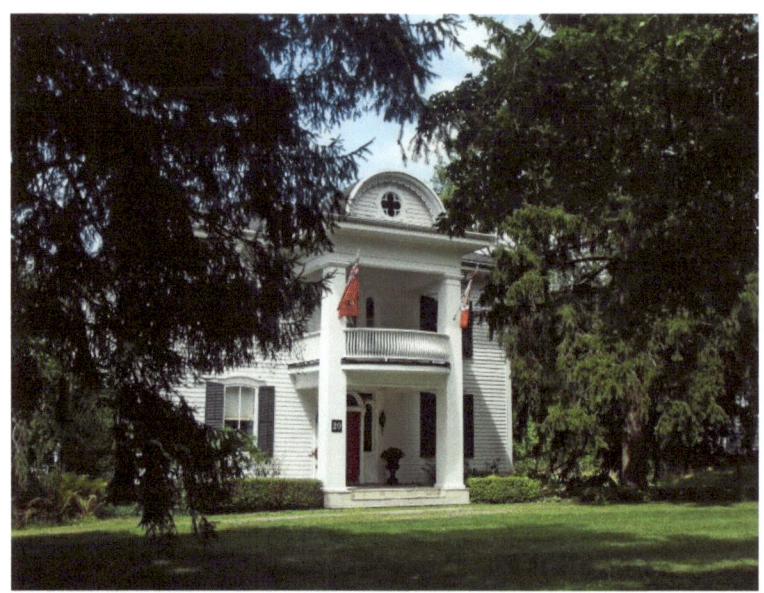

#20 Margaret Street – built 1871 – majestic two-storey
Georgian frame house with Italianate bracketing

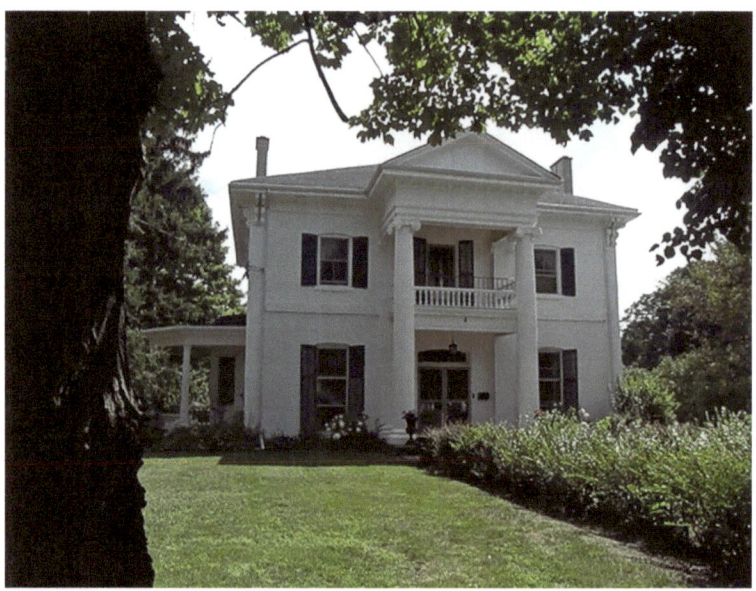

Italianate – verandah with two-storey Ionic pillars with
pediment, cornice brackets

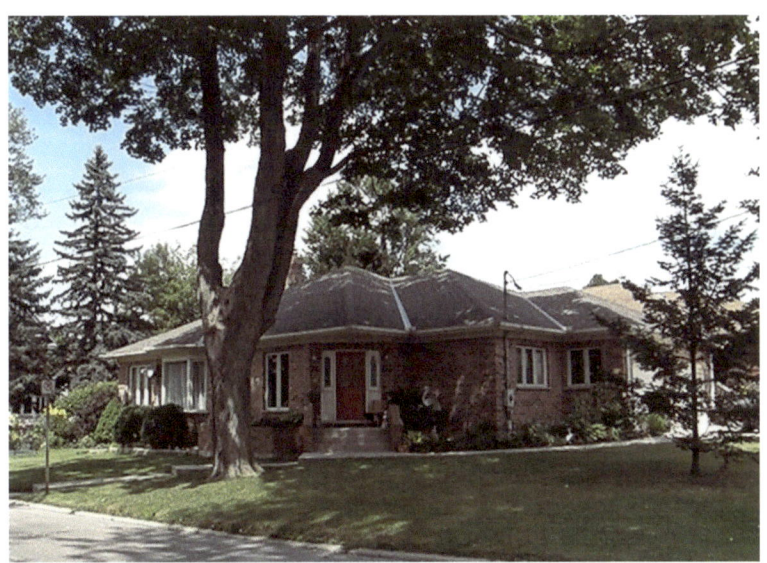

One storey – hipped roof

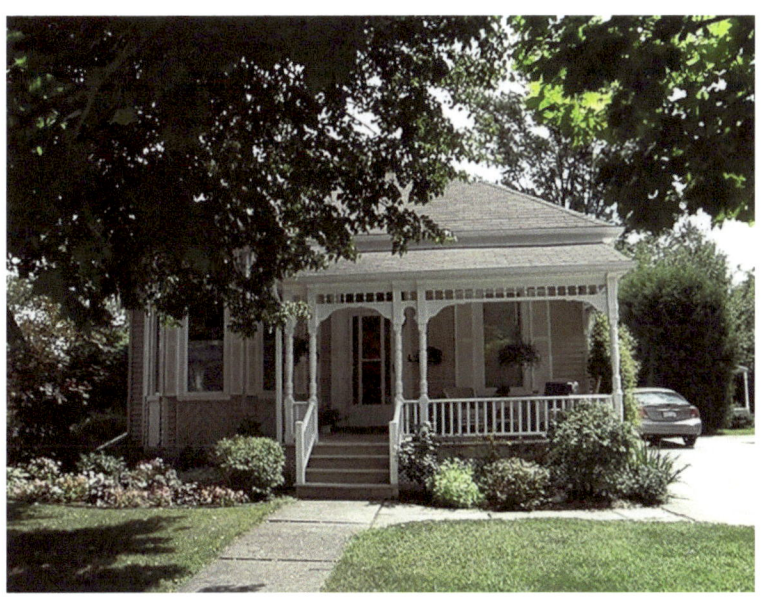

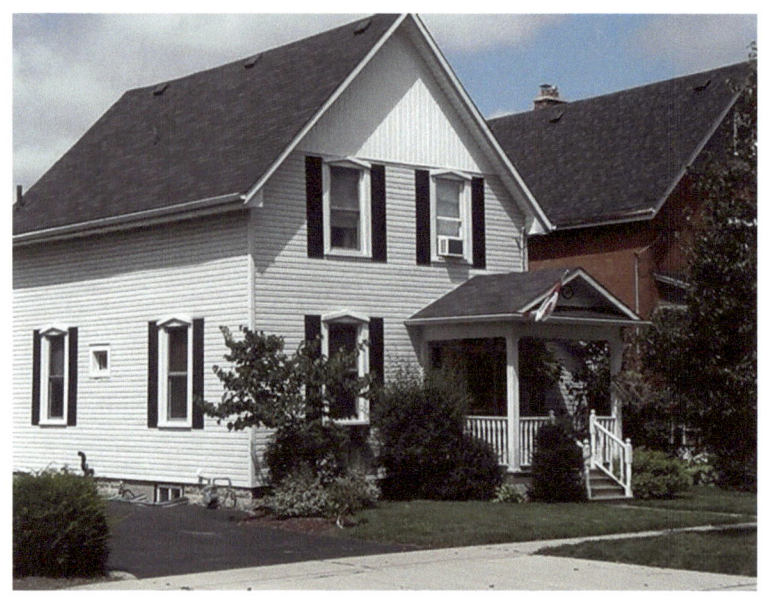

Gothic Revival – pediment above verandah

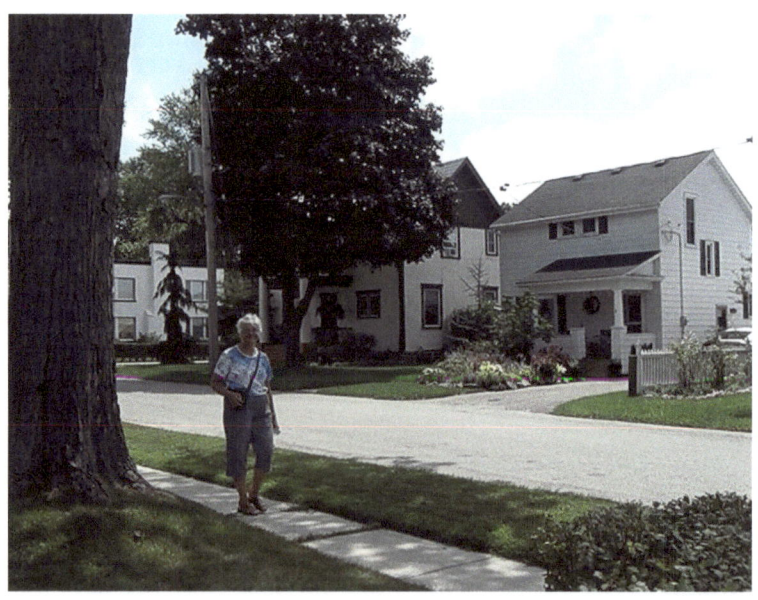

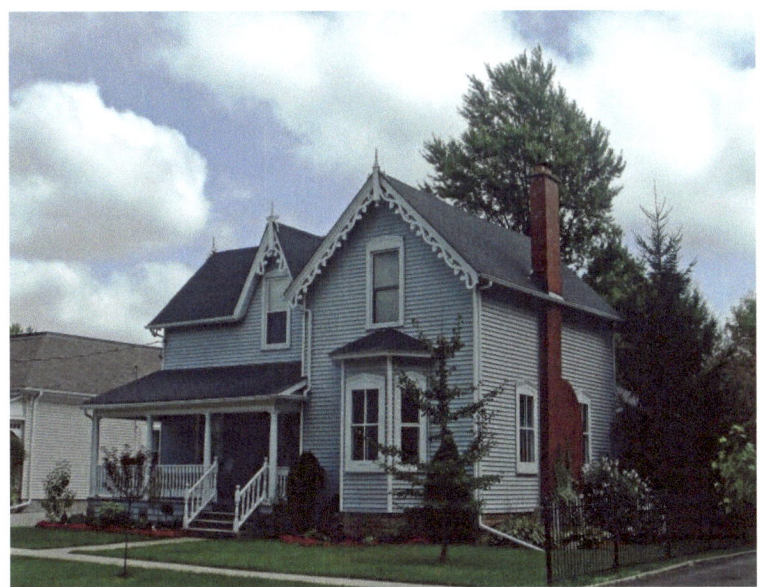

25 Margaret Street – built 1875 – two-storey frame Gothic Revival – elaborate scrolled Vergeboard trim with finials on gables, projecting wing with a three windowed bay

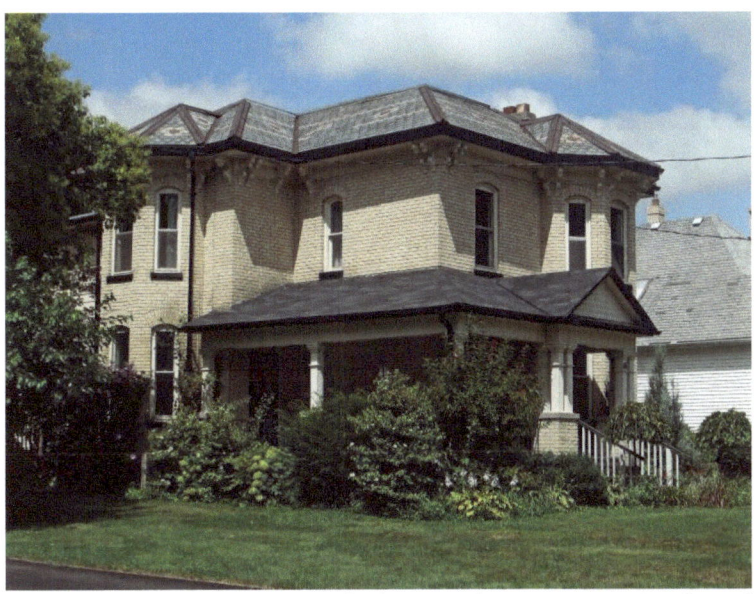

Italianate – trichromatic roof tiles, pediment, cornice brackets

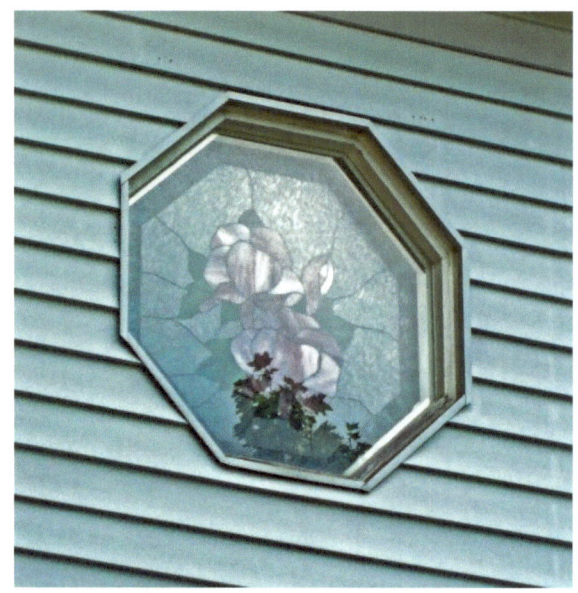

Stained glass window

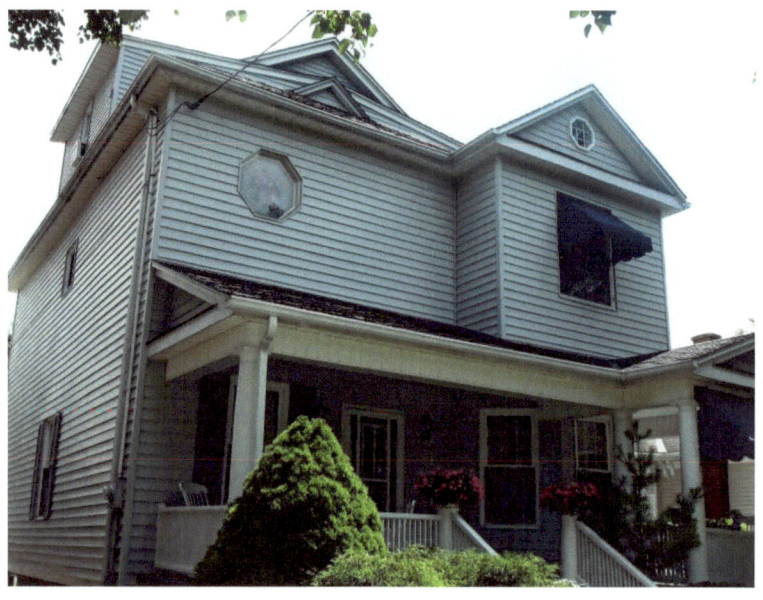

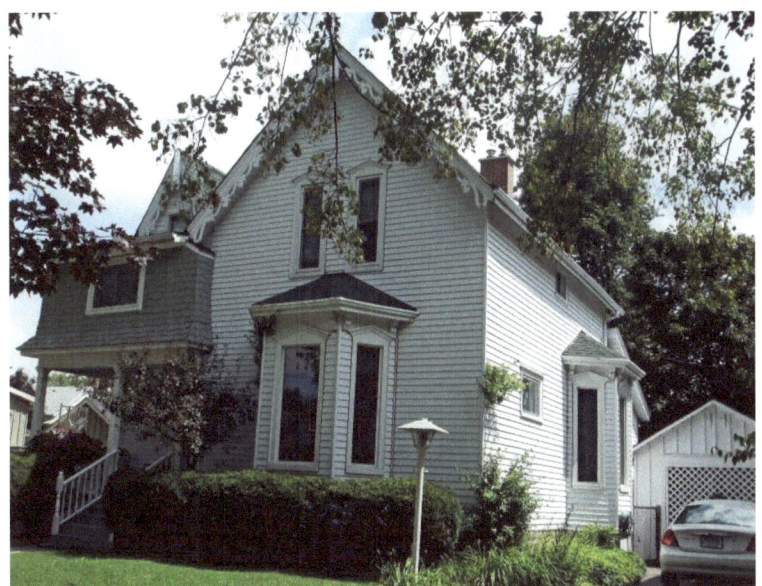

13 Margaret Street – built 1878 - Gothic Revival – scrolled
Vergeboard trim, three-window bay

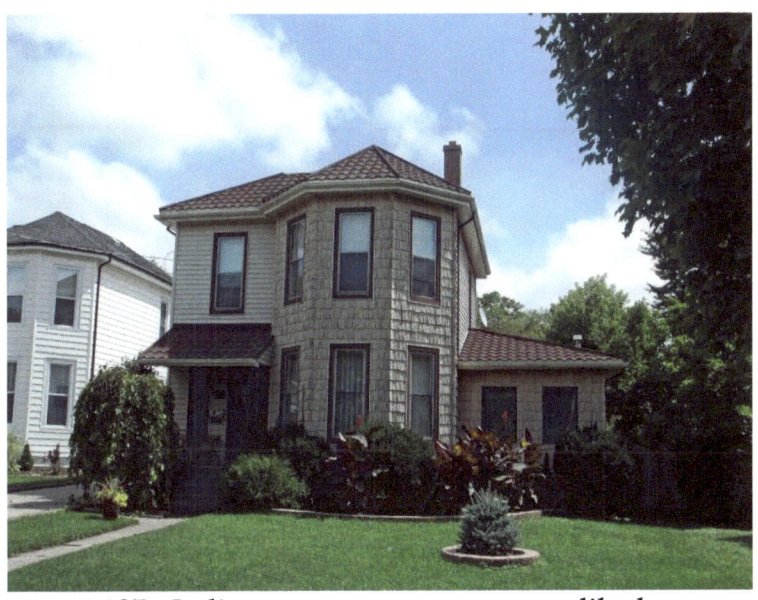

105 - Italianate – two-storey tower-like bay

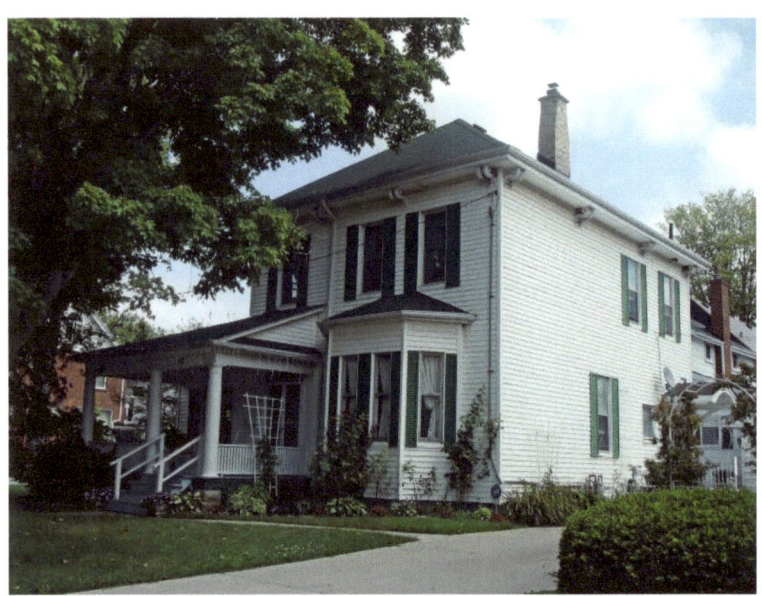

#95 - Italianate – hipped roof, paired cornice brackets

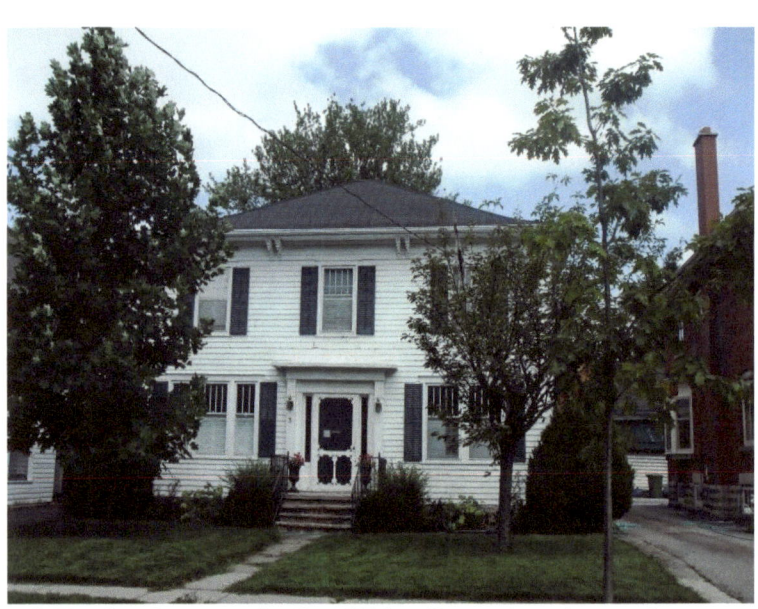

3 Drake Street – built 1876 – Georgian frame house
– paired cornice brackets

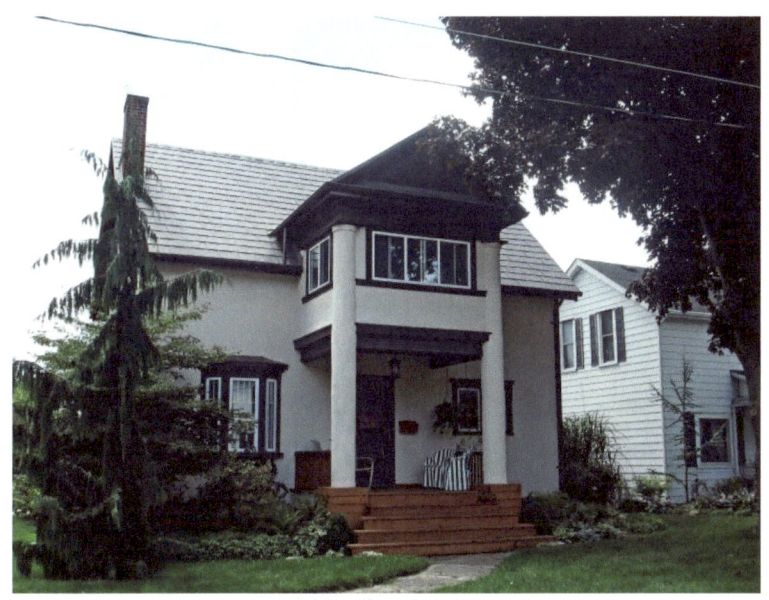

4 Drake Street

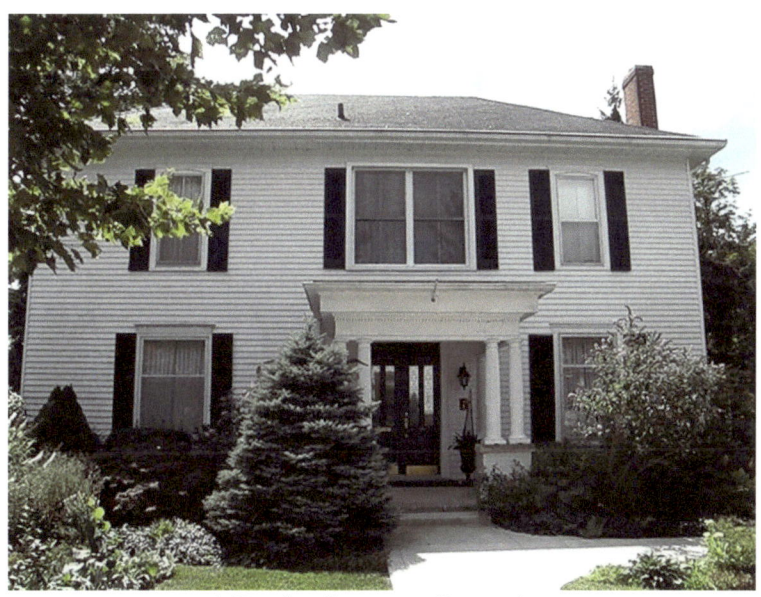

6 Drake Street - Georgian

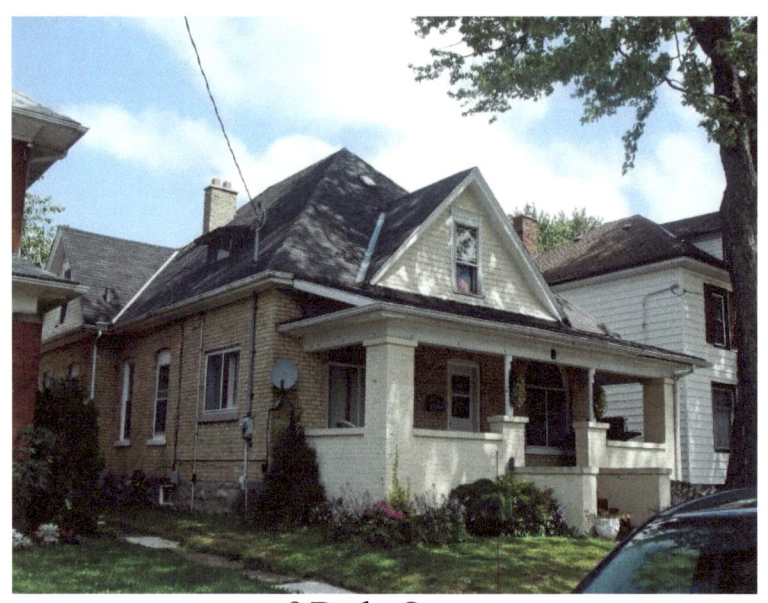

9 Drake Street

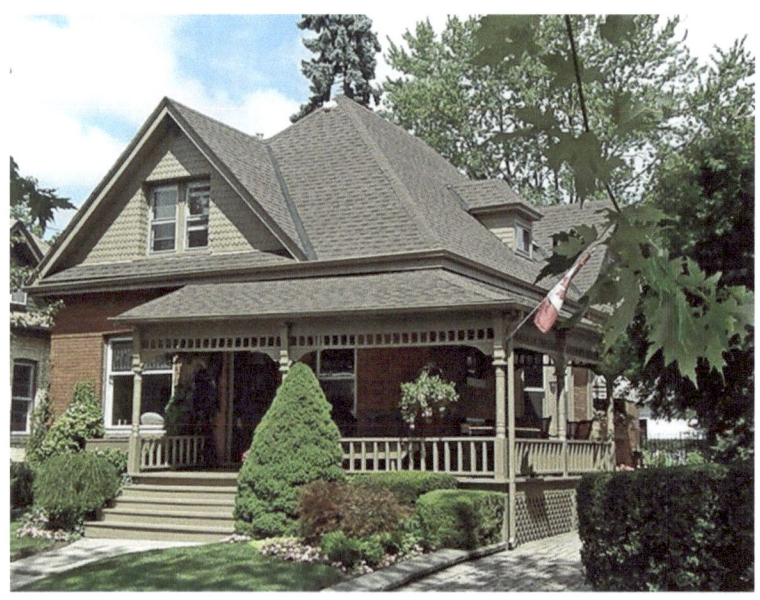

Port Stanley

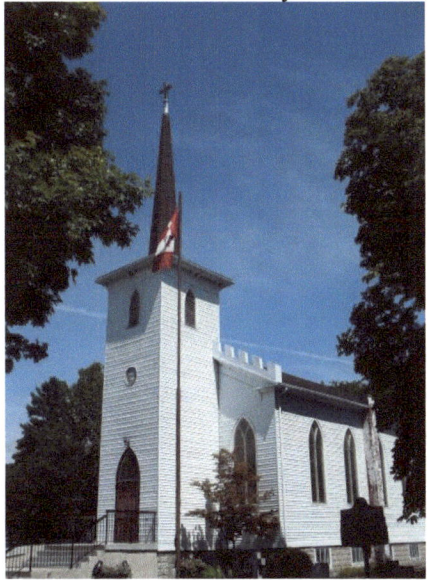

Christ Church – Anglican – 1845

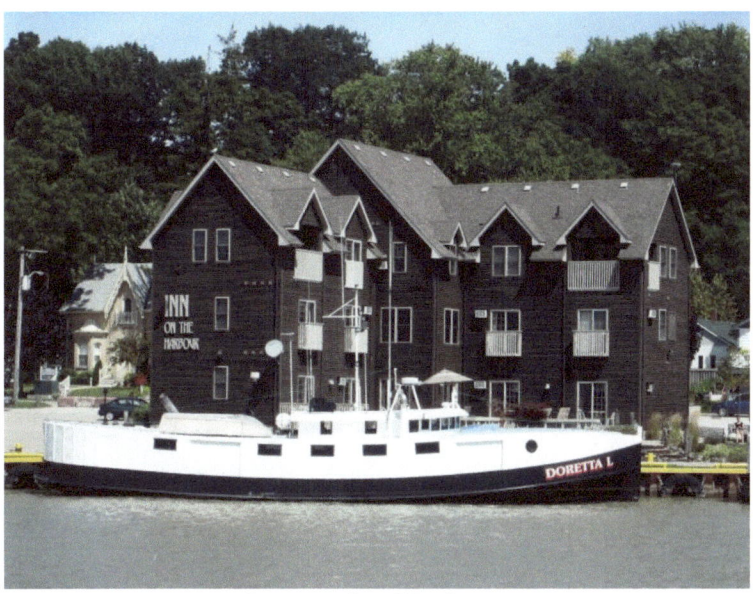

Inn on the Harbour

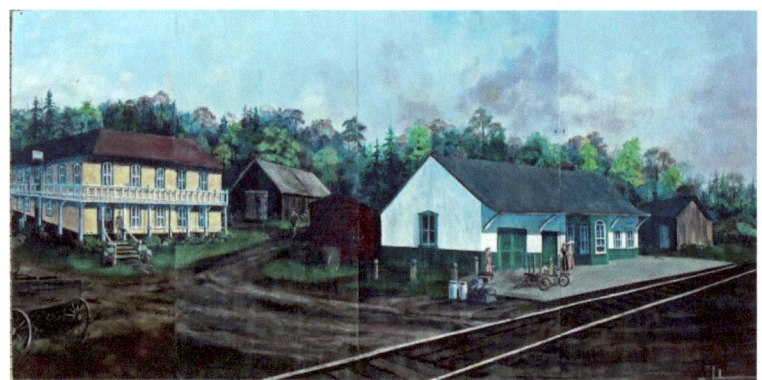

Mural

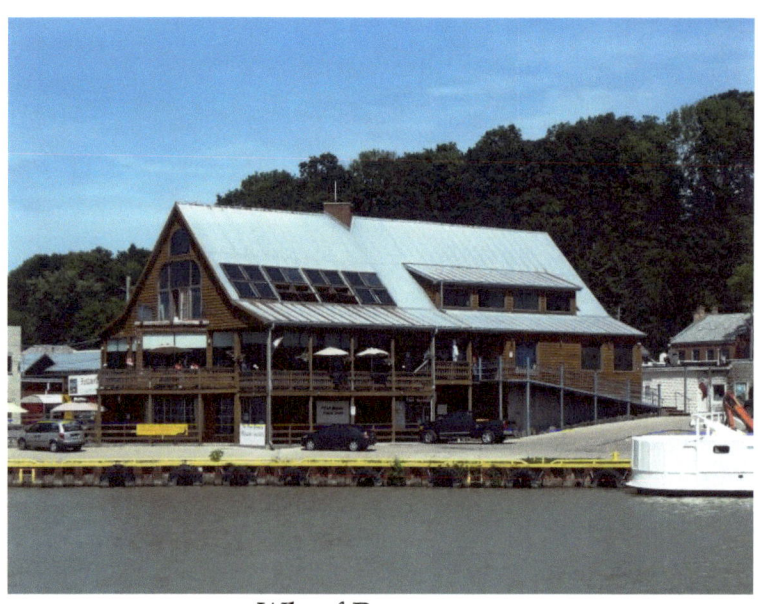

Wharf Restaurant

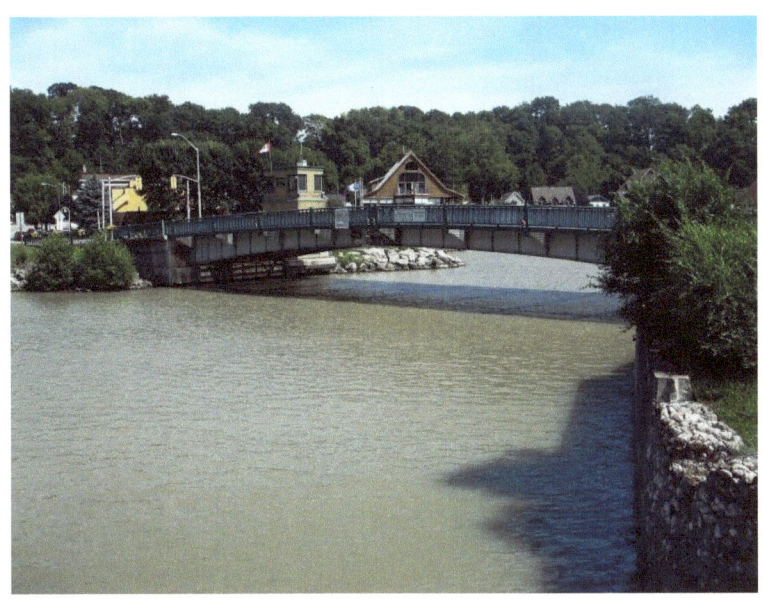

King George VI lift bridge, meandering Kettle Creek

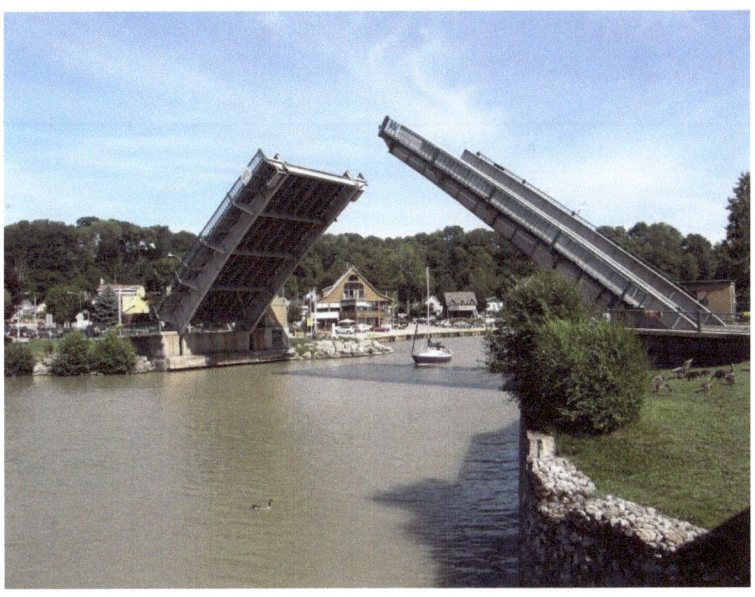

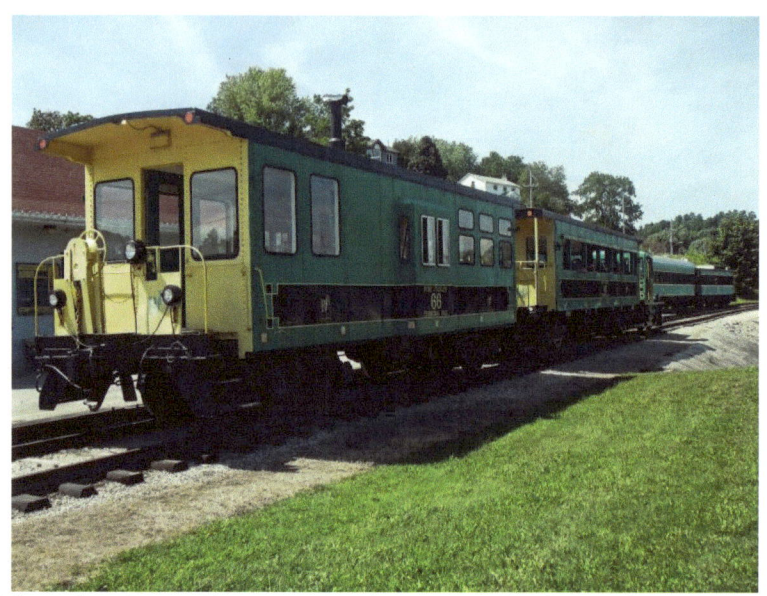

After the Great Western Railway reached London in 1853, local businessmen and politicians began promoting a competitive line south to Lake Erie. The London and Port Stanley Railway began operations in 1857. It shipped coal from Pennsylvania and carried tourists to and from the lakeshore. We took a ride into the countryside.

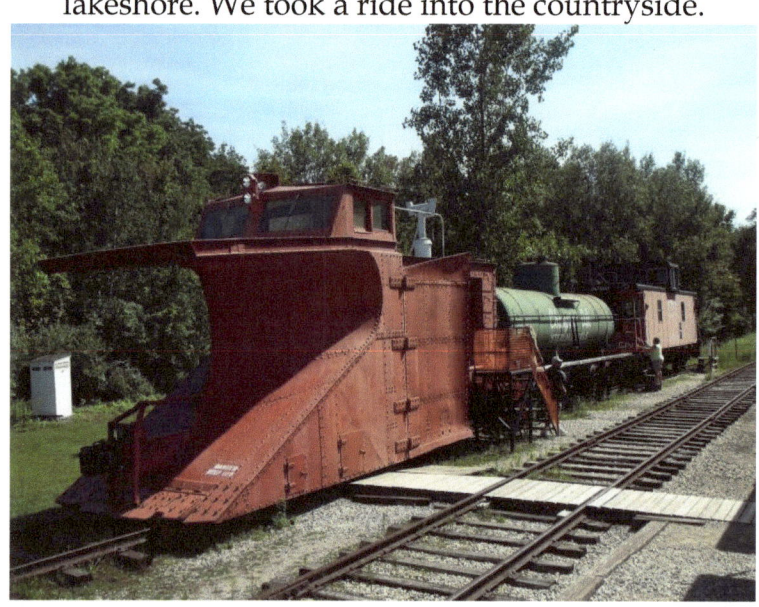

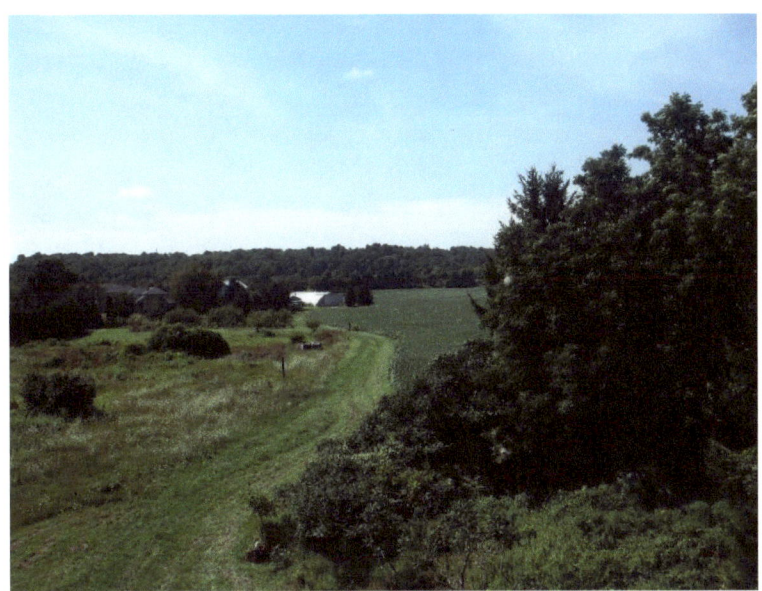

A view from the train

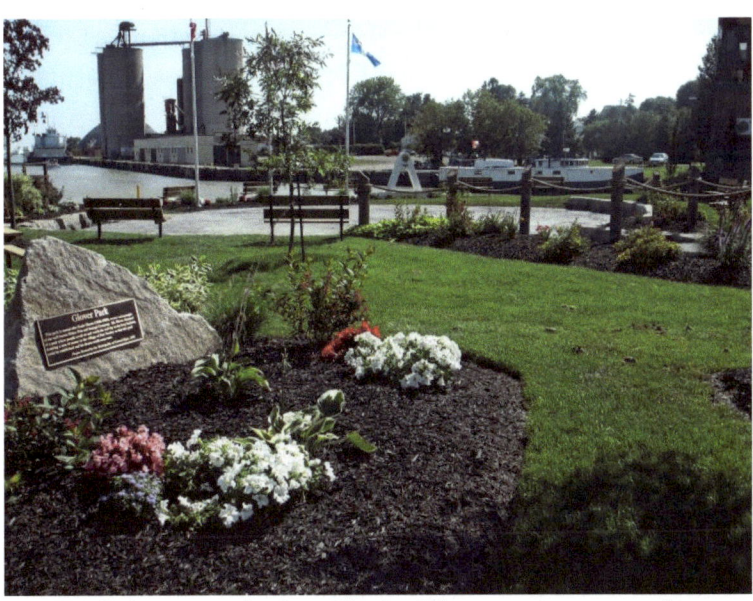

Glover Park is named after Ernie Glover, owner and manager of Finlay Fish and Storage Company. Mr. Glover dreamed of a park where people could sit and watch the activity in the busy harbour. He donated money to the village for this park.

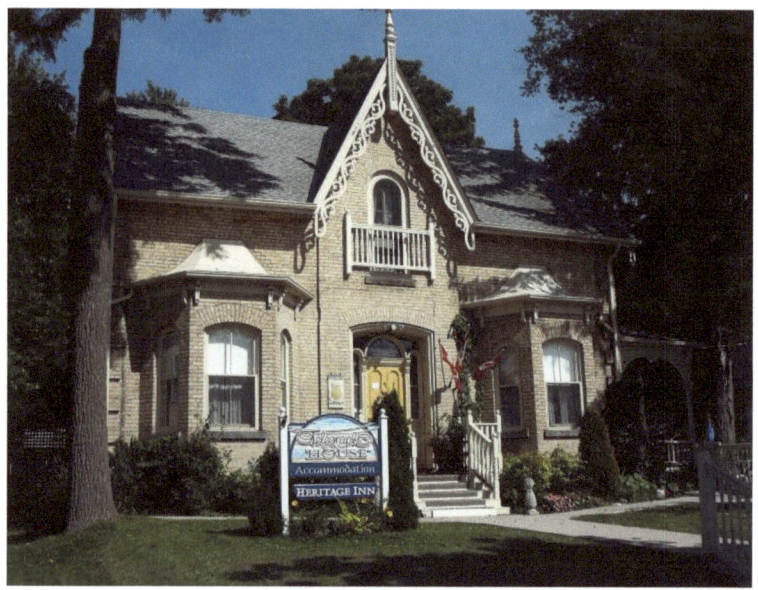

Telegraph House is an example of early Victorian architecture, lovingly restored to its former elegance. Constructed of the yellow brick popular in the region in the late 19th century, the Telegraph House presents a pleasing symmetry of form with its prominent bay windows, distinctive ornate dormer and elegant central hall design. The house was built in 1873 by Manuel Payne on the foundation of John Bostwick's original home. Bostwick, Port Stanley's first settler, subsequently moved to the crest of the hill overlooking the village, but the remnants of the original foundation of his home remain inside the foundation of this house. Manual Payne was an important resident of the village, serving as post master for over 40 years, reeve, customs agent, express agent, telephone operator and issuer of marriage licenses. It is fitting that the present owners chose to name their Bed and Breakfast the Telegraph House since Payne was the telegraph agent for Port Stanley as early as 1865, and played a vital role in connecting the little village to the rest of Canada West.

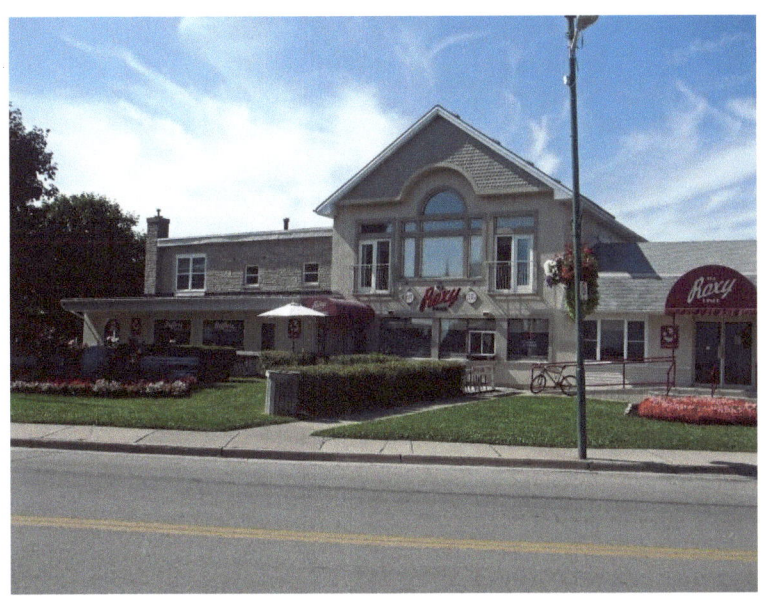

We had dinner at Roxy Restaurant.

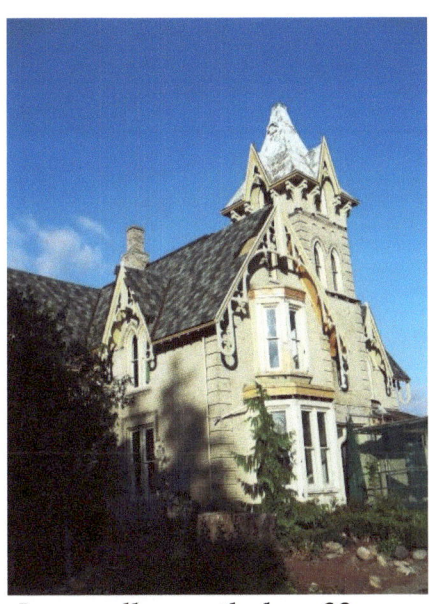

Elm Hurst Inn, Ingersoll – nestled on 33 acres – built in 1872
Queen Anne style

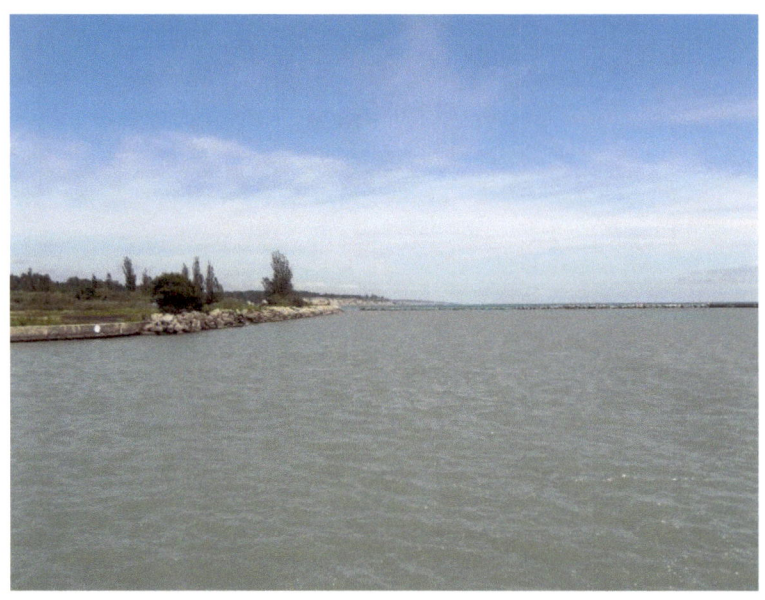

Port Stanley has one of the finest stretches of sandy beach on
the north shore of Lake Erie.

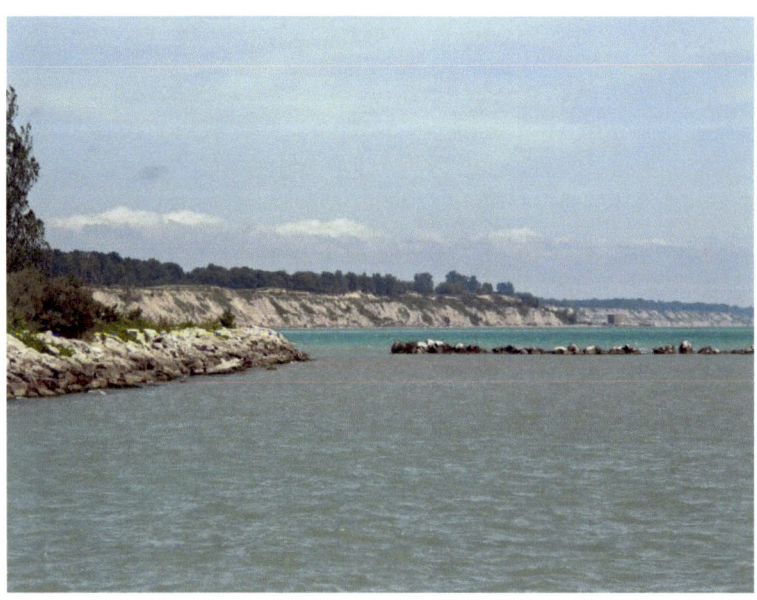

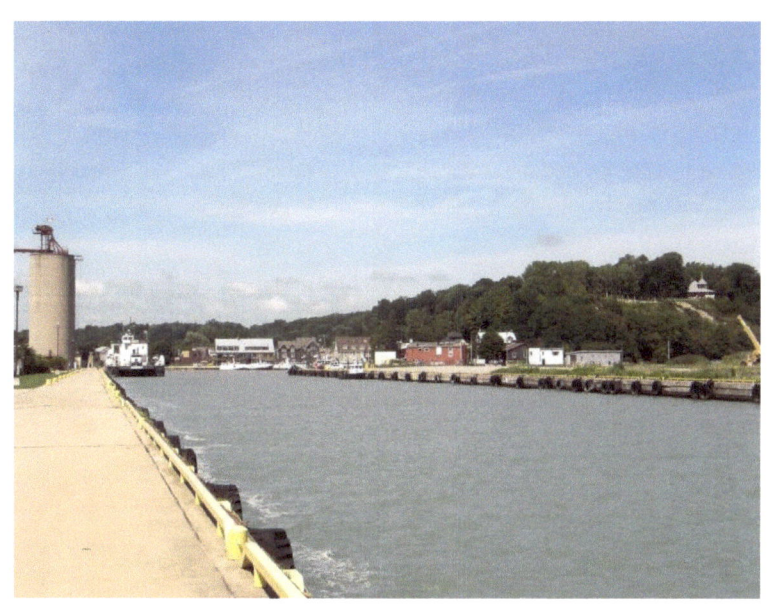

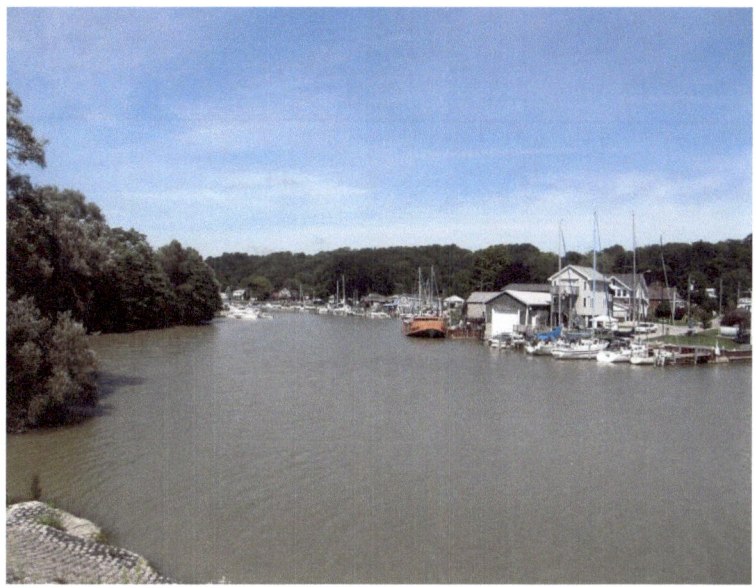

Brackets: a decorative or weight-bearing structural element which forms a right angle with one side against a wall and the other under a projecting surface such as an eave or roof. Example: 9 Wellington Street, St. Thomas	
Cornice: originally the wooden overhang of the roof. With the use of stone, brick, iron and steel, the cornice is any projecting shelf at the top of a ceiling or roof. They can be very decorative. Example: St. Thomas	
Dichromatic brickwork: the use of two colours of brick, tile or slate to decorate a façade. Trichromatic – three colours.	
Dormer: (French for "sleep") a gable end window that pierces through the plane of a sloping roof surface to create usable space in the top floor or attic of a building by adding headroom. Example: St. Thomas	
Frontispiece: a portion of the façade of a building, usually a centred doorway that is slightly raised from the rest of the building, usually has extensive ornamentation. Frontispieces are usually Classical in design with white columned porches.	
Gable: the triangular portion of a wall between the edges of a sloping roof. Example: 72 Metcalfe Street, St. Thomas	

Hipped Roof: a roof where all sides slope downwards to the walls with no gables.	
Keystones and Voussoirs: a voussoir is a wedge-shaped element used in building an arch. A keystone is the central stone that locks all the stones into position, allowing the arch to bear weight. A keystone is often enlarged and embellished. Example: St. Thomas downtown	
Pediment: a triangular section above the horizontal structure (entablature), typically supported by columns. The inside of the triangle is called the tympanum.	
Vergeboard and Finial: also called bargeboards – hang from the projecting end of a roof and are often elaborately carved and ornamented. **Finial:** ornament added to the top of a gable, pinnacle, canopy or spire – a Gothic element. Example: 25 Margaret Street, St. Thomas	

Edwardian, 1900-1930 – This style bridges the ornate and elaborate styles of the Victorian era and the simplified styles of the 20th century. Balanced facades, simple roof lines, dormer windows, large front porches, and smooth brick surfaces are its characteristics. Example: Metcalfe Street, St. Thomas	
Georgian, before 1860 – This style began with the British King Georges in the 18th century. These buildings have balanced facades around a central door, medium-pitched gable roofs, and small paned windows. Example: 6 Drake Street, St. Thomas	
Gothic Revival, 1830-1890 – These decorative buildings have sharply-pitched gables with highly detailed vergeboards, pointed-arch window openings, and dichromatic brickwork. It is a common style in Ontario. Example: 72 Metcalfe Street, St. Thomas	
Italianate, 1850-1900 – It has wide-bracketed eaves, belvederes, wrap-around verandahs. Example: 91 Metcalfe Street, St. Thomas	

Queen Anne, 1885-1900 – This style is distinguished by an irregular outline featuring a combination of an offset tower, broad gables, projecting two-storey bays, verandahs, multi-sloped roofs, and tall, decorative chimneys. A mixture of brick and wood is common. Windows often have one large single-paned bottom sash and small panes in the upper sash. Example: 1 Wellington Street, St. Thomas	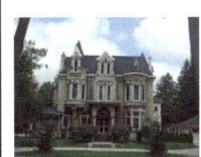
Romanesque Revival, 1880-1910 – This style hearkens back to medieval architecture of the 11th and 12th centuries with a heavy appearance, blocky towers and rounded arches.	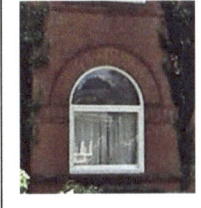

www.ingramcontent.com/pod-product-compliance
Lightning Source LLC
Chambersburg PA
CBHW041145180526
45159CB00002BB/738